**Explore Your Watershed
Adventure Guide**

Adapted by: Marine CSI

Copyright © 2020 Marine CSI: Coastal Science Investigations
First edition, self-publication
ALL RIGHTS RESERVED

Table of Contents

Introduction 5

Barrier Islands/Barrier Beaches 7

Maritime Forests 15

Salt Marshes 23

Lakes and Ponds 31

Urban Centers 39

Bibliography 47

THIS BOOK IS MADE FOR:

_____

INTRODUCTION

We all love being outside, running through tall grass, and playing hide-and-seek through the trees.

We love skipping rocks across ponds, and finding the best sticks to hike with.

We love going beyond our backyards and exploring what else is out there.

Now there's a way for you to explore even more places. These activities will give you a closer look into what and who is out there.

So, grab your parents and head outside! Let's have an adventure to each of the unique habitats along our coast!

WHAT IS A WATERSHED?

A watershed is all the land that funnels water down to its lowest point. The lowest point could be a major river or an estuary or even the ocean. The highest part of the watershed could be a mountain range or small rolling hills.

The Mississippi River Watershed collects water from many different states, but the Cape Cod Watershed collects water from several counties within one state.

Can you name which watershed your house belongs to?

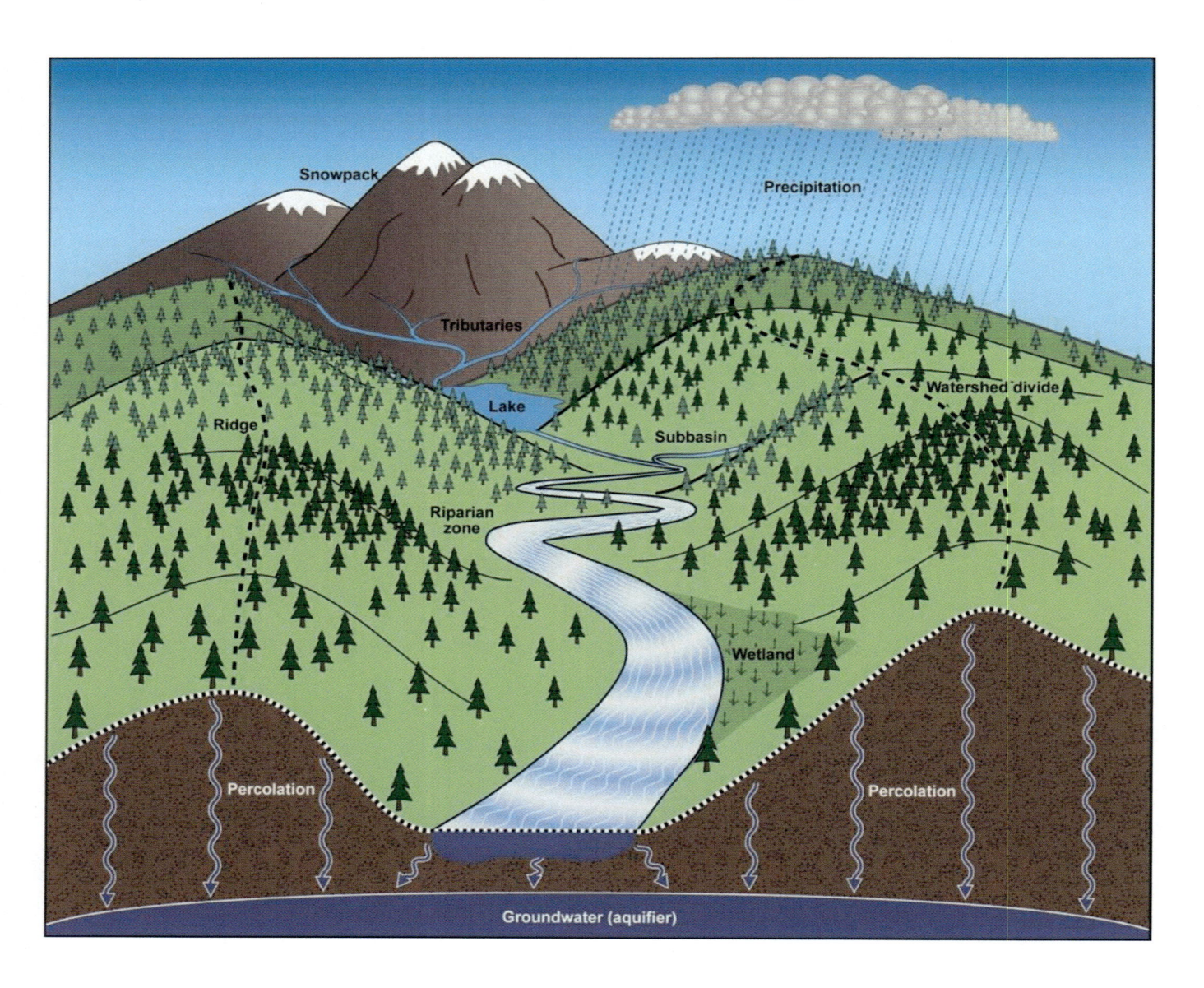

BARRIER ISLANDS/BARRIER BEACHES

Barrier islands are different from other islands because they are made from waves and storms, not from volcanoes.

They hug the coastline and act like a safety barrier, catching the impact from the fiercest waves and wind before the storms hit the mainland.

DID YOU KNOW?

Barrier beaches are made of sand grains, minerals, and skeletons of invertebrates.

Surfers   **Sand Castles**   **Sea Turtles**   **Seals**

DID YOU KNOW?

Dune plants have roots called rhizomes, which are very close to the surface to absorb water.

BARRIER ISLAND PLANTS

What You Need: Paper, pencil, measuring tape, clipboard

What To Do:
1. Go to any public beach access that has a wooden walkway and mark the measuring tape at three feet. This is approximately one meter.

2. Beginning at the base of the dunes, ask an adult to help you hold the measuring tape for each set up three feet intervals.

3. Look out at the dunes in front of you. Between the two ends of the measuring tape, count how many stems of one plant species you see.

4. Write down the number on your paper as Plant 1, Plant 2, Plant 3, etc. Then move on to the next three feet, and then the next.

5. Do you see a pattern forming of the number of plant stems as you move across the dunes? Do you see a pattern of the number of plant species you find?

This is called **dune succession** and as you move away from the water, you will see more and more species. A plant field guide will help you figure out which species you saw.

| American Beach Grass | Prickly Pear Cactus | Beach Morning Glory | Large-leaf Pennywort |

BARRIER ISLAND ANIMALS

What You Need: bucket, shovel

> *DID YOU KNOW?*
>
> Some animals that live on a barrier island bury themselves under the sand for protection.

What To Do:
1. Take your bucket down to the "wrack line" where all kinds of shells have washed up onto the beach.

2. Collect as many shells as you can fit in the bucket and bring them back to your blanket or beach chair.

3. Clean off most of the sand from each shell and organize them by size, shape, color, and texture.

4. See if found any shells like clams or mussels that have a hinge which holds them together. Did you find any shells attached to each other?

5. Further divide your shells into those you think have two shells and those you think only have one shell.

When you divide animals based on their size, shape, color, and texture, it is called **taxonomy**.

Scientists around the world use this to group animals that are similar to each other and name them.

Ghost Crabs **Coquina Clams** **Gray Foxes** **Least Sandpiper**

DID YOU KNOW?

Soil on the barrier island is dry and washes away quickly, creating scarps on the beach.

BARRIER ISLAND SOILS

What You Need: sandwich baggies, shovel, Sharpie

What To Do:
1. Label four sandwich baggies – dunes, backshore, foreshore, and nearshore – with the Sharpie (or get an adult to help you).

2. Access the beach from any public access area and stop at the base of the dunes. Use your shovel to take a small sand sample.

3. Walk a little bit towards the ocean and stop. The sand is much hotter here, but take a sample and put it into the backshore baggie.

4. Find the wrack line, where all the shells and driftwood are. Take a sample here, putting it into the foreshore baggie.

5. At the water's edge, right before you get to where the water is coming up, take your last sample of sand. Place it into the nearshore baggie.

6. Compare the sand from each area of the beach. Which sand grains are coarse and look more like pebbles? Which ones are fine and look more they've been ground up really small?

Fine sand has been worn down by waves, wind, and storms. This is called **weathering**. Weathering happens more in areas where there are a lot more storms.

Sand Dunes **Wrack Line**  **Sand Minerals**  **Beach Erosion**

WATER ON A BARRIER ISLAND

WHAT YOU NEED: tennis ball, clipboard, measuring tape, paper, pencil, watch

DID YOU KNOW?

Water on a barrier island is salty and comes from ocean waves and tides.

What To Do:
1. Go to an uncrowded part of the beach. Take the measuring tape and mark out 10 feet in the sand.

2. Standing on one mark, throw the tennis ball into the water, past the waves breaking on shore.

3. Using your watch, time how long it takes the tennis ball to go from the first mark to the second mark, at 10 feet.

4. Record this time (in seconds) on your paper.

5. Using this formula, calculate how fast the tennis ball was going:

$$\text{Speed (feet per second)} = \frac{10 \text{ feet}}{\text{Time}}$$

The tennis ball does not come back to the same spot you threw it, just like when we swim in the ocean, we may come out of the water far from our blankets/chairs. This is called the **longshore drift**. It is caused when waves crash on an angle to the shore.

| Waves | Inlets | Hurricanes | Storms |

USE YOUR SENSES

> *DID YOU KNOW?*
>
> A change in temperature at the beach is because wind blowing off the water is often cooler.

What You Need: your ears

What To Do:
1. Access the beach from any public access area and walk down to the water's edge.

2. Sit down on the sand and close your eyes.

3. Concentrate on the waves in front of you as you listen closely to when they crash down on the sand.

4. Keep your eyes closed and see if you can use your ears only to picture the waves crashing in your mind.

5. Concentrate real hard and you will also see the waves crashing down on either side of you.

You can visualize something without using your eyes because your senses are stronger when one or more are blocked. By blocking your sight, your ears work harder to hear the image instead of see it.

TAKE ACTION!

What You Need: bucket, gloves, garbage bags

> *DID YOU KNOW?*
>
> The International Coastal Cleanup is held in September every year all over the world.

What To Do:
1. Take your bucket down to the wrack line, where all the seashells and driftwood are.

2. Using your protective gloves, pick up any trash you find in between the shells.

3. Place any regular trash into the garbage bags. These can be deposited into the trash bins along the beach or the parking lots.

4. Place any recyclable items such as plastic, glass, aluminum, and paper into the bucket. If there is a recyclable bin in the parking lot near the beach, deposit them there. If not, you can recycle them at home.

Recycling is one of the best ways we can help our planet. Some items, such as glass and plastic, take a really long time to break down or **biodegrade**. This means that they stay in their original form and can do more harm to plants and animals after we use them.

BARRIER ISLAND FIELD GUIDE

What You Might Find on a Barrier Island

DID YOU KNOW?

Barrier islands move every year because sand is deposited and eroded at each end.

Sea Oats	Goldenrod	Beach Heather	Little Bluestem
Whelks	**Sand Dollars**	**Mussels**	**Sand Crabs**
Sea Stars	**Brown Pelicans**	**Herring Gulls**	**Oystercatchers**

-- 14 --

MARITIME FORESTS

Maritime forests are formed over time, as seeds from plants are moved by birds and other animals.

> **DID YOU KNOW?**
>
> Maritime forests, or marine forests, are found on barrier islands or close to an estuary.

Most of them don't have people living on them and it's a great place to see wildlife in their natural habitat. A lot of animals blend in with their surroundings, so you have to look real hard to find them.

Forest Path **Freshwater Marsh** **Hawks** **Turtles**

DID YOU KNOW?

Plants of the maritime forest have shallow roots to absorb water quickly before it's gone.

MARITIME FOREST PLANTS

What You Need: paper, pen, clipboard, plant field guide

What To Do:
1. Stop at different places along a trail through the forest and identify three species of trees in each area. Write their name down on the paper or draw them to identify later.

2. Using the species as your guide, determine whether you are in the uplands, lowlands, or tidal creek area of the maritime forest.

3. Write down one special feature of each plant. This could be the type of bark, leaf shape, length of trunk, or where it is located in the forest compared to other plants.

4. Search for a tree that has fallen down or snapped in half. If you can get to it safely, count the rings to determine how old it was.

As you go from the uplands to the tidal creek, this is called **forest delineation**. You will see different species in different areas because of their ability to handle salt water and salt spray from the ocean.

| Live Oaks | Pines | Ferns | Maples |

MARITIME FOREST ANIMALS

> **DID YOU KNOW?**
>
> Animals that live in maritime forests are hidden, but we find signs of them everywhere.

What You Need: camera, paper, clipboard, colored pencils

What To Do:
1. On your walk through the forest, keep on the lookout for what might be an animal home.

2. Use tracks in the soil to direct you to certain places where an animal might be hiding.

3. If you brought a camera with you, take a picture of what you see, making sure you capture all the details around it, like whether it's on the ground, in the trees, or between two trees.

4. If you can't take a picture of it, use the paper and colored pencils to sketch it out. You don't have to be an artist to draw what you see!

5. Can you guess which animal belongs in which home you found?

Animals find many ways to hide from predators, including people. Sometimes they blend in with their surroundings. This is called **camouflage**. Animals will use this when they are away from their homes and still need to be protected.

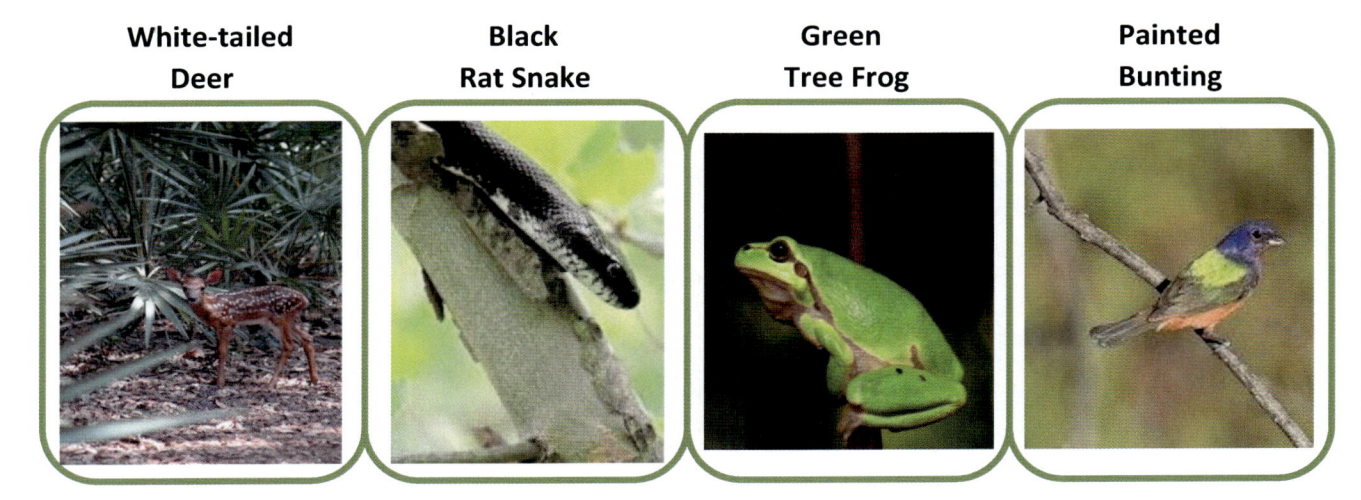

White-tailed Deer	Black Rat Snake	Green Tree Frog	Painted Bunting

DID YOU KNOW?

Maritime forests transition between sand dunes and salt marsh, so their soils can vary.

MARITIME FOREST SOILS

What You Need: 3 glass jars, coffee filters, shovel, paper, pencil, clipboard, water

What To Do:
1. As you walk through the maritime forest, look down at the ground and notice the soil changing. This natural transition alerts you that you are in the uplands, lowlands, or tidal creek areas of the forest.

2. In the uplands, set up your soil sample experiment. Take the coffee filter and place it over the top of the open glass jar.

3. Shovel a small sample of soil onto the coffee filter.

4. Pour some water over the soil, allowing it to filter through the soil and into the jar. How much water has filtered through this type of soil?

5. Repeat these steps for all three soil types. Which soil filtered the water best? How much water did you get from each area?

When soil has lots of minerals, it is called **nutrient-rich**, and is really great for growing many species.

When soil is **nutrient-poor**, like that found closest to the beach, not many plants can grow there.

| **Sandy Soil** | **Leaf Litter** | **Minerals** | **Pine Straw** |

-- 18 --

WATER IN A MARITIME FOREST

What You Need: measuring tape, paper, pencil, clipboard, shovel

DID YOU KNOW?

Vernal ponds are bodies of water that appear when there's nowhere else for water to go..

What To Do:
1. Head towards the uplands part of the maritime forest first. Find a spot that is safe to stand in slightly off the trail.

2. Using the shovel, dig a small hole in the soil. Notice what color it is, whether it has minerals, and how thick it is.

3. Continue digging down until the soil gets very moist or you find water.

4. Use the measuring tape to find out how deep the hole is. Record the number on your paper and label it Uplands.

5. Repeat steps 2 – 4 in the lowlands and tidal creek areas and record the numbers on your paper.

6. Compare the numbers. Which area had water that was deeper? Which area had water that was shallower or closer to the surface?

When water goes down into soil, it **infiltrates**. That means it gets down in between the soil particles until it can't go any further and forms a pool of water underground.

Vernal Pond   **Freshwater Swamp**   **Salt Spray**   **Rain Water**

-- 19 --

> *DID YOU KNOW?*
>
> Different birds will live in different parts of the maritime forest. Just listen for their calls.

USE YOUR SENSES

What You Need: your ears, binoculars

What To Do:
1. As you walk through the maritime forest, you will start to hear birds and other animals around the trees.

2. Using your ears first, listen closely to the tops of the trees and the ground around the shrubs.

3. Once you hear something, use your eyes in the direction of the sound.

4. If you don't see something right away, keep looking. If you spot an animal, use the binoculars to get a closer look at it.

5. What type of animals did you hear? What type of animals did you see? Were the animals different as you got to different areas of the maritime forest or were they similar throughout?

Binoculars are like glasses or contacts but they have magnifying glasses inside them. They help to center your attention on one thing at a time and bring it closer to your eyes so you can see something in more detail.

TAKE ACTION!

What You Need: your eyes, binoculars, Great Backyard Bird Count Checklist, pencil, clipboard, bird ID list

> *DID YOU KNOW?*
>
> Building bluebird nest boxes helps to keep the mosquitoes away since they eat them.

What To Do:
1. Have an adult go on the internet and print out the new year's Great Backyard Bird Count checklist. This special weekend comes around every February.

2. Go out to the nearest maritime forest and write down the name of the place on the checklist sheet.

3. Using your eyes first, look up to the top of the trees for any birds that may be sitting on branches.

4. Once you spot one, use the binoculars to get a closer look at the bird.

5. Use the bird ID list to try to identify the species you discovered and check them off the Great Backyard Bird Count checklist.

6. Spend as much time as you can out in the maritime forest checking off as many birds from the list as you can.

7. Have an adult go back onto the Great Backyard Bird Count website and add your list to the site.

The Great Backyard Bird Count is put together by the National Audubon Society and Cornell University every year. There are so many bird species that our help is needed to identify and count them. This is called **citizen science**. You got to be a scientist for a day!

MARITIME FOREST FIELD GUIDE

What You Might Find in a Maritime Forest

DID YOU KNOW?

Looking at a maritime forest from a beach, the trees get taller because there's less salt.

- American Holly
- Red Cedar
- Sassafras
- Wax Myrtle

- Box Turtle
- Glass Lizard
- Five-lined Skink
- Cardinal

- Black and White Warbler
- Red-tailed Hawk
- Bald Eagle
- Eastern Cottontail

SALT MARSHES

DID YOU KNOW?

Salt marshes are shallow bodies of water that act as nurseries for baby crabs and fish.

Salt marshes may be the healthiest habitat that we have along our coasts, due to the plants filtering water from nearby rivers.

Every coastal area surrounding our country has a salt marsh and estuary, with the largest one near the Gulf of Mexico.

| Kayaking | Bird Watching | Fishing | Crabbing |

DID YOU KNOW?

Salt marsh plants take up nutrients in their roots and clean the water of pollution.

SALT MARSH PLANTS

What You Need: measuring tape, paper, pencil, clipboard

What To Do:
1. On the paper, write the words "grasses," "shrubs," and "trees."

2. Move safely over to the edge of a marsh platform, where you can see the water clearly.

3. Use the measuring tape to measure the length of a few grasses, from the base to the tip. Write those numbers down on the paper.

4. Where you see the first shrubs, measure the length of a few shrub plants. Write those numbers down on the paper.

5. Move closer to the forest edge. Measure the length of a few short trees. Write those numbers down on the paper.

6. Which plants are longer in length? Why do you think they are longer where they are located on the marsh platform?

The **marsh platform** extends from the forest edge to the water's edge. Tides and streams will bring soil to the platform until it is built up and seeded with different species over time.

Turtle Grass   **Cordgrass**    **Glasswort**    **Mangroves**

SALT MARSH ANIMALS

What You Need: shovel, sieve, bucket, water shoes

> *DID YOU KNOW?*
>
> Salt marsh animals can regulate their bodies for both salt water and freshwater.

What To Do:
1. When you enter a salt marsh, make sure that the mudflat is exposed and you are at low tide.

2. Shovel mud onto the sieve and shake it so the mud and sand particles fall out, leaving only larger things, like shells and animals.

3. If you need help getting the mud out of the sieve, use some water from the creek.

4. Any animals you find hiding in the mud, place in the bucket. Can you name them?

5. Can you describe why these animals are found in the mud instead of up near the plants? Are they vertebrates or invertebrates?

6. Make sure you place all the animals back in the mud or in the water after you have identified them.

Animals that live in the **mudflats** protect themselves from the sun and salt when the tide goes out and the mud is exposed. Some will bury themselves, others will tightly close their shells.

Fiddler Crabs   **Oysters**   **Terrapins**   **Seahorses**

DID YOU KNOW?

Salt marsh soils contain salt from the water when the tides come in from the ocean.

SALT MARSH SOILS

What You Need: two or more people, sneakers, measuring tape

What To Do:
1. Walk out safely onto a salt marsh platform.

2. Use the measuring tape to measure out 10 feet. Split your group in half, so that some are at the 10 feet mark and some are at the 0 feet mark.

3. On the count of three, the people at the 10 feet mark jump at the same time. Do the people at the 0 feet mark feel the vibrations?

4. Measure out 5 feet and repeat step 3. Do they feel the vibrations this time?

5. Measure out 3 feet and repeat step 3. Did they feel the vibrations? What was different about it this time?

6. Measure out 1 feet and jump. Did the people at the 0 feet mark feel the vibrations more?

The reason you feel vibrations in the soil when you jump is because salt marsh soil is very moist and spongy. This soil is called **peat** and is made up of water, roots of live plants, and decaying dead plants.

Mudflats **Hammocks**  **Sandy Bottom**  **Tides**

WATER IN THE SALT MARSH

What You Need: dip nets, safety jackets, sneakers, buckets

DID YOU KNOW?

Water in the salt marsh is brackish, a mix of salt water and freshwater.

What To Do:
1. Walk to a public marina or boat dock that you can easily get to safely.

2. Lie flat on your stomach on the dock. Use your dip net to scrape off some of the animals clinging to the dock. Put them in your bucket.

3. Try to catch a few fish, being careful not to stretch out too far over the dock.

4. Are the animals you are collecting vertebrates (with backbones) or invertebrates (without backbones)?

5. Was it easy or hard to scrape the animals off of the dock?

6. Take a look at the different species you collected. What do they have on their bodies that helps them stick to the sides of the dock and not float away with the tides?

Animals that attach to hard surfaces, like docks and the bottom of boats, are called **sessile** or immobile. Some have shells to protect them. They have to wait for food particles in the water to come to them when the tides go in and out every day.

| Tidal Creeks | Rivers | Oceans | Clouds |

> **DID YOU KNOW?**
>
> When the mud is exposed, animals will either escape to the water or bury further down.

USE YOUR SENSES

What You Need: your nose

What To Do:
1. Go out to the salt marsh during high tide (when the water is up to the grasses). Make sure you can safely walk out onto a marsh platform.

2. Close your eyes and take a deep breath in. What do you smell? Does it smell like the ocean or something else?

3. Go out to the salt marsh during low tide (when the water is low enough to expose the mud). Make sure you can safely walk out to the marsh platform and not get stuck in the mud.

4. Close your eyes and take a deep breath in. What do you smell? Do you smell the ocean or something else?

5. Why do you think it smelled different between high tide and low tide?

High tide is when the waters from the ocean enter into a salt marsh through a creek or river. They are pulled up into the marsh by the force of the moon on Earth. **Low tide** is when ocean water is pulled back out towards the ocean by the force of the moon on Earth.

TAKE ACTION!

What You Need: kayak/canoe, oars, life jacket, camera

What To Do:
1. Safety first! Make sure your life jacket is securely on before you get into a canoe or kayak.

2. Head out into the creeks surrounding the marsh hammocks (islands).

3. Using your camera, document your trip through the salt marsh. Take a picture of your boat in the water, the mudflats, the grass on top of one of the marsh hammocks, and a bird.

4. If you are able to get close enough without disturbing them, take a picture of a crab crawling on the mud.

5. Challenge yourself and see if you can take a picture of every type of animal living in the salt marsh habitat.

DID YOU KNOW?

By planting native plants in your yard, you use fewer nutrients, keeping them out of the marsh.

When we say **leave only footprints**, it means we are not disturbing wildlife in any way. We are not throwing our trash onto the ground or in the water, we are not chasing after the birds to make them fly, and we are only leaving our footprints behind so there is no sign we were even there.

SALT MARSH FIELD GUIDE

What You Might Find in a Salt Marsh

DID YOU KNOW?

Salt marsh hammocks erode faster due to and sea level rise and global climate change.

Sea Lettuce

Red Algae

Sea Oxeye

Widgeon Grass

Marsh Crabs

Killifish

Grass Shrimp

Mud Snails

Horseshoe Crabs

Worms

Quahog Clams

White Ibis

- - 30 - -

LAKES AND PONDS

Freshwater lakes and ponds can be found from the mountains to the coast.

> **DID YOU KNOW?**
>
> Lakes and ponds are found further inland but are still part of the coastal watershed.

Lakes are larger than ponds and much deeper. The fish that live in those ecosystems are also larger and freshwater fishing is a popular sport there.

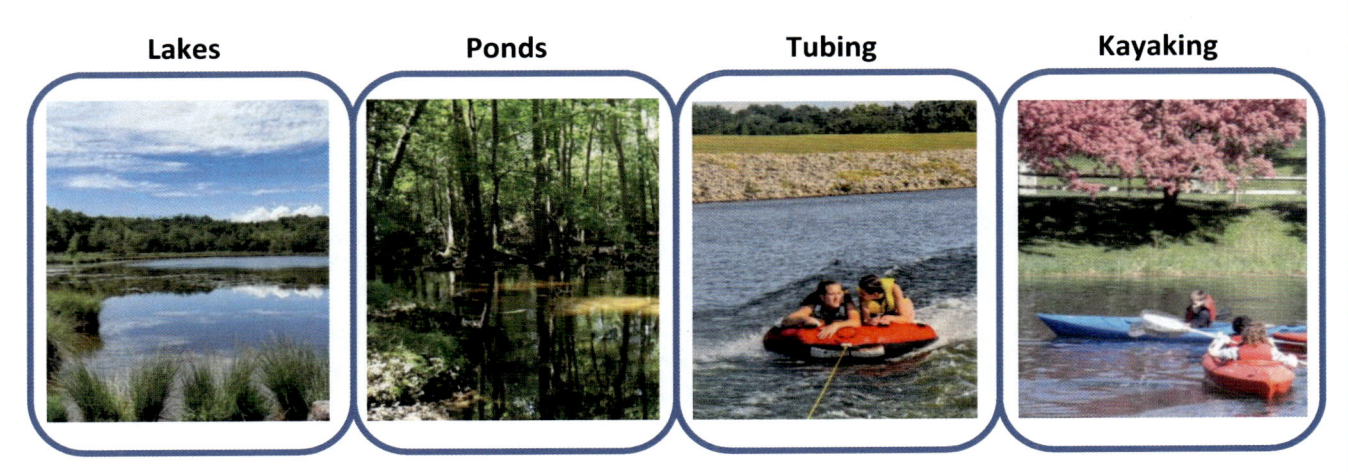

| Lakes | Ponds | Tubing | Kayaking |

DID YOU KNOW?

Most plants in lakes are found around the banks because their roots can reach the bottom.

LAKES AND PONDS PLANTS

What You Need: pencil, clipboard, water shoes, canoe or kayak, life jacket

What To Do:
1. Fold your paper in half from top to bottom. Label the top half Lake and label the bottom half Pond.

2. Safely walk around the edge of the first body of water and either name or draw the plants that you find. Try to be as specific as possible and ask for help with their names.

3. With an adult, use either a canoe or kayak to paddle out towards the middle of the pond or lake.

4. Name or draw the plants that you see in the middle, if there are any.

5. Is there a difference in the number of plants around the edge or the species between a pond and a lake? Is there a difference in the number and species in the middle?

A great **indicator species** is the water lily. If you find them throughout the body of water, not just around the edges, it will most likely be a pond.

Pickerelweed　　**Cypress** 　　**Water Lilies** 　　**Common Reeds**

LAKES AND PONDS ANIMALS

What You Need: home-made aquascope, water shoes, extra clothes, towel

> *DID YOU KNOW?*
>
> Some lakes and ponds are stocked with fish each year so that we can catch them for fun.

What To Do:
1. Have an adult make your aquascope: Take a plastic container, cut a big circle out of the bottom, and cut a big circle out of the lid. Put a piece of plastic wrap over the top of the container and then put the lid back on tightly.

2. Find a safe area to walk into a lake or pond. Turn your aquascope upside down, so the lid with the plastic wrap is in the water.

3. Stick your eyes down into the open hole to view the plants and animals that might be swimming or crawling around. Turn over rocks and stones and see what could be living underneath.

4. What do you see? The plastic wrap magnifies things, or makes things look bigger, so you see more clearly.

A telescope magnifies things in the night sky that are too far away to see. A microscope magnifies things that are too small for our eyes to see normally. An **aquascope** magnifies things underwater.

| Brook Trout | Snowy Egret | Alligator | Beaver |

DID YOU KNOW?

When trees are cut down, their roots don't hold the soil, and it erodes and fills the water basin.

LAKES AND PONDS SOILS

What You Need: sieve, collection jar, extra clothes, towel, water shoes

What To Do:
1. Go to a local lake or pond and search for a small creek or tributary that enters into it.

2. Carefully, and with guided help, wade into the water with your sieve.

3. Dig up some of the sand and gravel and put it into the sieve. Give it a good shake, careful to only allow the sand to come out of the holes.

4. If you need to get more sand out, shake it under the water's surface. The water will loosen it enough to come out of the holes.

5. What you have left over could be minerals, parts of animals, like shark teeth or shells, or even gemstones.

6. Anything that is not alive you may put into your collection jar and take home with you.

Over time, a pond or a lake will get more soil from the surrounding rivers and streams. This soil comes in layers, called **horizons**, and they may contain fossils, minerals, or rocks that have been broken apart by water.

| Sand | Gravel | Detritus | Clay |

WATER IN LAKES AND PONDS

What You Need: water shoes, towel, canoe and oars, life jacket

> *DID YOU KNOW?*
>
> Water in lakes and ponds can come from the clouds or from underground wells, or aquifers.

What To Do:
1. With an adult, canoe out to the middle of the body of water and stop rowing. Are you still moving? What do you think is making you move?

2. Canoe to an area where a stream meets the lake or pond. When you stop rowing, do you still seem to move? What do you think is causing you to move?

3. Observe the weather. Is the wind calm or is there a slight breeze? Do you see wind moving across the surface of the water making ripples? Is the wind strong enough move your canoe?

4. Are there any other boats in the water with you? Are those boats creating ripples in the water that might be pushing your boat along?

5. Could an animal move your canoe? Is there an animal big enough in the lake or pond that might be able to move your canoe without touching it?

When water from the bottom of a lake or pond is stirred up by boats, wind, or an animals, it is more **turbid**. That means it is less clear and you cannot see down to the bottom.

| Streams | Snow and Ice | Underground | Man-made |

-- 35 --

DID YOU KNOW?

Water near the surface of a lake is usually warmer from the sun, so many fish are found there.

USE YOUR SENSES

What You Need: your hands, eyes, and ears

What To Do:
1. The best time to discover a lake or pond is during the changes of the seasons. Choose either winter to spring or fall to winter to explore.

2. If you choose winter to spring, use your hands to touch the ground near the water. Does it still feel hard and cold or is it beginning to soften to allow plants to grow?

3. If you choose fall to winter, use your eyes to view the changing colors of the leaves and count how many of them fall to the ground while you are there. Come back once a month to see how many more leaves are on the ground.

4. During these changes in seasons, there are a lot of migrating species that will come to a lake or pond to rest or feed. Use your ears to hear the differences in the number of birds or the types of calls they make during the different seasons.

5. What major differences do you see in the lake or pond community between the seasons?

Migration is when an animal flies, swims, or crawls from one area to another over a period of a few weeks to a few months. Depending on where they start and where they finally stop, this migration could be hundreds of miles from place to place.

TAKE ACTION!

What You Need: fishing pole, freshwater fish ID card, fishing license, life jacket

> **DID YOU KNOW?**
>
> Lakes and ponds can dry up or fill up based on the amount of rain or drought in the area.

What To Do:
1. Have an adult research a local lake or pond and see when there will be a kids-only fishing tournament.

2. Make sure you have the right fishing license to participate in the tournament and remember to register before the event.

3. During the tournament, make sure you are only keeping what you are allowed to keep and place the others back in the lake or pond.

4. How many did you catch? What species did you catch? Remember to tag the fish you are keeping so the authorities can keep track of how many fish are in the body of water each season.

When you keep track of how many of one species are in an area, that is called a **population count**. Scientists use this number to determine how many licenses they will allow year to year and how many fish each person is allowed to take.

DID YOU KNOW?

Some of our largest lakes were created when glaciers melted and boulders cut deep holes.

LAKES AND PONDS FIELD GUIDE

What You Might Find in a Lake or Pond

Cattail	Duckweed	Arrowhead	Purple Loosestrife
Mallard Ducks	Mute Swans	Loons	Bullfrogs
Snails	Painted Turtles	Carp	Bluegill

-- 38 --

URBAN CENTERS

DID YOU KNOW?

Many communities have created greenways to coexist with wildlife in urban areas.

The greatest number of people live within cities, places that are highly developed with lots of houses, stores, and roads.

The easiest way to get some fresh air is to bring plants into your home. They give you oxygen while taking in the carbon dioxide you breathe out.

Parks　　**Gardens**　　**Streets**　　**Playgrounds**

DID YOU KNOW?

Some plants are spread by seeds in the wind, while others are planted by humans.

URBAN CENTERS PLANTS

What You Need: paper, pencil, clipboard

What To Do:
1. Fold the paper in half so you have a right side and a left side. On the left side, write Trees. On the right side write Cars.

2. Start at your front door. Look out towards the street. Are there any cars parked there? Are there any trees there?

3. Walk around your whole block and count the number of trees and the number of parked cars. Keep a tally on your paper.

4. It takes ten trees to absorb the amount of air pollution put out by one car. In your tally, circle groups of ten trees.

5. Count how many groups you've circled and put that number at the bottom of the page. How does this number compare to the number of cars you counted? Is there enough trees for every car on your block?

Trees use **photosynthesis** to take in carbon dioxide from us and our cars. It cleans the air so we can breathe oxygen better.

Maple   **Dogwood**   **Dandelions**   **Flower Pots**

-- 40 --

URBAN CENTERS ANIMALS

What You Need: stop watch/timer, friends, cones or flags

> *DID YOU KNOW?*
>
> Animals in urban areas are so used to humans, you can see them outside during the day.

What To Do:
1. Get together with a group of your friends at a small park or an area with lots of wildflowers.

2. Have an adult set up the cones or flags across the field of flowers.

3. Each one of you will pretend to be a bee. Move from flower to flower, touching each one. Go to the far cones/flags and come back, touching flowers the whole time.

4. Have an adult time you with a stop watch as you race to be the first bee to pollinate all the flowers.

Bees and butterflies are very important animals because they pollinate flowers. **Pollination** is how flowers get their seeds to each other. Since flowers are rooted into the ground, they need help. Some flowers, like dandelions, use the wind, while others, like daisies, use bees and other flying insects.

Squirrels **Peregrine Falcons** **Raccoons** **Butterflies**

DID YOU KNOW?

In urban centers, soils often contain concrete, asphalt, and even pet waste.

URBAN CENTERS SOILS

What You Need: paper, pencil, clipboard, map of your town

What To Do:
1. Take a look at the map of your town and circle all the parks or green areas you can find.

2. Go to two parks closest to your house with an adult.

3. Fold the paper in half from top to bottom. On the top half write Park 1 and on the bottom half write Park 2.

4. At Park 1, go to the playground. What is the ground around the equipment made of? Is it sand, mulch, rubber, or something else?

5. Look outside the playground area. What is the ground made out of? Is it sidewalk, is there a garden with soil, or is it a different material?

6. Compare the first park to the second one, answering the same questions. Which park do you think is better for wildlife and people?

When the material on the ground allows water to drain down into it after it rains, it is said to be **permeable**. This type of material is better to catch pollution before it goes into a major waterway, like a lake or river nearby.

Topsoil	Coal Ash	Construction Debris	Bedrock

-- 42 --

WATER IN URBAN CENTERS

What You Need: paper, pencil, clipboard

> **DID YOU KNOW?**
>
> Some plants in urban centers have deeper and larger roots in order to reach water.

What To Do:
1. Start at your front door and walk all the way around your block until you reach your front door again.

2. Using your paper, draw a map of your block, labeling the streets, and using squares to represent the buildings.

3. On the streets, draw out where there are storm drains, places where water flows when it rains.

4. On the buildings, draw out where the rain gutters are and whether rain flows into a garden or onto the sidewalk.

5. How many gutters move water directly from the roofs of the buildings to the streets and storm drains? How many of them go into gardens or into the ground?

When rain from the roofs of buildings goes into gutters and then onto the streets, it is called **runoff**. Runoff can be bad for nature because it collects garbage, chemicals, and debris from houses, sidewalks, and roads.

Ponds   **Rain Gutters**   **Storm Drains**   **Sprinklers**

> **DID YOU KNOW?**
>
> Where you find trees, you will find wildlife. Just look on branches or inside trunks.

USE YOUR SENSES

What You Need: bubbles, a windy day

What To Do:
1. Take your bubbles outside. Blow a few bubbles in front of your house. Which direction do they go? Does the wind take them away quickly or slowly? Do they stay bubbles or do they pop right away?

2. Move around the corner from your house, where there is a street. Blow the bubbles again. What does the wind do with the bubbles now?

3. Try going to different areas of your neighborhood to blow bubbles.

4. Does the wind blow the bubbles in the same direction at each location?

5. Do the buildings change the direction of the bubbles? Does the street make the bubbles move faster or slower?

Wind tunnels are created when wind is squeezed into a narrow space, like the space between two buildings. As the space gets smaller and smaller, wind is pushed faster and faster through.

TAKE ACTION!

What You Need: paper, pencil, clipboard, colored pencils

> *DID YOU KNOW?*
>
> Rain gardens use native plants to hold soil better and they're great for pollinators too.

What To Do:
1. Hold your clipboard sideways and at the top of the paper write My Neighborhood.

2. Starting with your house, draw a map of your neighborhood, at least five blocks or so long. You can go bigger if you'd like.

3. Include in your map any buildings, streets, traffic lights, parks, and trees. Make it as detailed as possible. You can use symbols if the pictures are too big to fit on one paper.

4. When your map is done, look at how much of your neighborhood is covered with trees or grass or other types of plants.

5. Do you think there is enough in your neighborhood or do you think there should be more? If you can, find a safe spot near your house to plant a sapling of a tree or other native plant and watch it grow.

DID YOU KNOW?

Urban centers are now a great place to grow a community garden for everyone to enjoy.

URBAN CENTERS FIELD GUIDE

What You Might Find in an Urban Center

| White Oak | Honey Locust | White Clover | Common Ivy |

| Brown Bats | Green Anole | Tent Caterpillar | Ladybugs |

| Canada Geese | Robins | Mourning Dove | Crow |

BIBLIOGRAPHY

BARRIER ISLANDS/BARRIER BEACHES:
New Jersey Sea Grant Consortium. "Classification and Identification." 2 March 2013.
<njseagrant.org/images/education/LessonPlans/classification_and_identification.pdf>

New Jersey Sea Grant Consortium. "Sand Sampling." 5 October 2012. <njseagrant.org/>

New Jersey Sea Grant Consortium. "Longshore Current." March 2014.
<njseagrant.org/up-content/uploads/2014/03/longshore_current.pdf>

MARITIME FORESTS:
Cornell University and National Audubon. "Great Backyard Bird Count." 23 May 2020.
<gbbc.birdcount.org>

SALT MARSHES:
U.S. Environmental Protection Agency. "Marshes." 10 October 2012. 16 April 2014.
<water.epa.gov/type/wetlands/marsh.cfm>

FRESHWATER LAKES/PONDS:
All For the Boys. "DIY Underwater Scope." 26 May 2020.
<allfortheboys.com/diy-underwater-scope/>

Inland Associated Press. "Using the 5 Senses to Discover Signs of Spring with Children."
19 March 2012. <inlandpress.org/stories/using-the-5-senses-to-discover-signs-of-spring-with-children.5033?>

URBAN CENTERS:
PBS Kids. "More Trees Please." Plum Landing. 29 May 2020.
<pbskids.org/plumlanding/educators/activities/more_trees_please_fam.html>

WHO WE ARE

MARINE CSI: COASTAL SCIENCE INVESTIGATIONS
Our Website: www.teachmarinecsi.com
Our Email: education@teachmarinecsi.com

FOR MORE COOL ACTIVITIES JUST FOR YOU:
www.teachmarinecsi.com/kids-page

FOR MORE ACTIVITIES YOU CAN DO WITH AN ADULT:
www.teachmarinecsi.com/sample-lesson-plans

Made in the USA
Columbia, SC
16 March 2021